Jason from
Grandpa & Grandma
Ross

Secrets
of
Animal
Survival

A mountain goat and her month-old kid peer over a cliff edge on Mount Evans, in Colorado. Their padded, hard-edged hooves give them firm footholds on steep rock, helping to keep the goats from falling. The design of the goats' hooves is one of the secrets of animal survival. Read about these and other goats in the chapter on mountains.

BOOKS FOR WORLD EXPLORERS
NATIONAL GEOGRAPHIC SOCIETY

COVER: *A giraffe nibbles a branch in Kenya, in East Africa. Read about giraffes in the chapter on savannas.*

M. P. KAHL

COPYRIGHT © 1983
NATIONAL GEOGRAPHIC SOCIETY
LIBRARY OF CONGRESS CIP DATA: PAGE 104

Introduction

Visit almost any part of the world, and you'll find animals of some kind living there. They swim in icy polar seas. They hop across broiling desert sands, and they swing through steamy tropical rain forests. They graze on vast savannas, or grasslands, and they climb among high, windswept mountains. These environments can be harsh, yet animals live in them. Their bodies and habits have adapted to their homes.

Scientists recognize several different types of environments worldwide. Each has its own climate and plant and animal life. Scientists call such an area a biome (BY-ome). In this book, you'll explore five biomes and meet some of the animals that live in them. You'll discover how the structure of an animal's body can help the animal obtain food, survive temperature extremes, escape enemies, and raise young.

POLAR REGIONS

On an Antarctic shore, emperor penguins soak up the sun (above). Although ice and snow cover much of Antarctica, strong winds sweep across slopes, keeping some higher areas almost clear of snow.

At the top and at the bottom of the globe lie two of the coldest regions on earth. These are the areas surrounding the North Pole and the South Pole. The northern polar region, the Arctic, consists of the Arctic Ocean and its bordering lands. Most of the land is tundra. The tundra, a vast, treeless area, supports grasses and blooming flowers in summer. The ground below the surface remains frozen all year, however. Melting snow cannot seep through the frozen earth, so the tundra becomes soggy in summer.

The frozen continent of Antarctica and the oceans around it make up the southern polar region. Antarctic mountains rise thousands of feet. Ice covers much of the land. In some places, the ice is nearly 3 miles (5 km)* thick. The temperature in Antarctica has plunged as low as minus 127°F (–88°C), making it the coldest place in the world.

*Metric figures in this book have been rounded off.

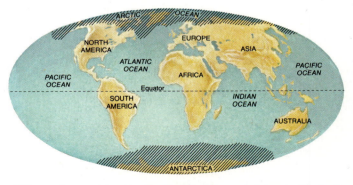

The polar regions, shaded by lines (above), include the North and South Poles. The northern region is called the Arctic; the southern, the Antarctic.

Mighty hunter, a polar bear (right) rears up and sniffs the air. It stands on the ice in Hudson Bay, in Canada. The polar bear hunts seals. Its white coat matches the ice and snow. This coloring helps the bear approach seals unseen.

Polar bear cubs tag along after their mother near an island off the coast of northern Norway. Polar bears usually give birth to two cubs, in midwinter. At birth, the cubs have almost no hair. Here, in the spring, the five-month-olds have grown thick hair, which protects them from the cold. The cubs will remain with their mother for about two years.

MARTIN ROGERS

Sniffing around, a polar bear peers from her den (above). In winter, female polar bears dig dens in snowbanks. There, they give birth to their cubs. Adult males spend the winter on frozen bays or seas.

Northern Hunter

The polar bear roams the Arctic and nowhere else. It lives along the treeless shores of Alaska, Canada, Greenland, Norway, and the Soviet Union. In search of food—mainly seals—the polar bear travels hundreds of miles a year through the Arctic. At different times of the year, it swims across long stretches of water and walks along barren shores or on frozen bodies of water.

The polar bear is a powerful swimmer. Its broad front feet, slightly webbed, paddle strongly. A narrow head, long neck, and sloping chest make this kind of bear more boat-shaped than other bears. The polar bear can swim dozens of miles through open water. On land or on ice, it can gallop at least 25 miles an hour (40 km/h). Hair around its foot pads helps the bear avoid slipping on the ice.

A polar bear uses its sharp claws to help it catch seals. In winter, seals underwater use breathing holes in the ice to reach *(Continued on page 10)*

A female polar bear rests in a den, curled up with two cubs. The female used her sharp claws to dig the den. It has two rooms. Drifting snow has covered the entrance. The snow keeps out cold winds. A narrow vent poked through to the surface lets in fresh air. The cubs were born in late December. Each was about the size of a guinea pig. The mother nurses her cubs in the den for three or four months. During that time, she eats no food. For nourishment, she depends on body fat stored in warmer months.

Churning through icy water, a polar bear (left) paddles with its front feet. Under its skin, a thick layer of fat, called blubber, keeps the bear warm. As a female bear leads her young ashore (below), water pours off their coats. The polar bears' fur sheds water easily. Shedding water prevents their coats from freezing.

(*Continued from page 7*) the air. A polar bear on the ice uses its keen sense of smell to find such a hole. Then it waits at the edge. When a seal surfaces, the bear takes a quick swipe with its paw. It often catches the seal with its claws and lifts it onto the ice.

Suited for Survival

Just as the polar bear is adapted for survival in its cold environment, so are the animals it hunts: the harp seal, the ringed seal, and the bearded seal. The harp seal spends most of its life in the icy water. Not all kinds of seals can survive the cold of the far northern waters. The adult harp seal, however, is protected from the cold by a thick layer of fat, called blubber, under its skin.

The harp seal feeds on fish. To catch its food, it swims fast and acrobatically. Its speed in the water also helps the seal escape from polar bears. On ice, a bear can catch a seal in a short chase. In the water, however, the bear is no match for the speedier seal.

The harp seal gives birth on the sea ice, where the young seal, called a pup, spends its first few

weeks. The pup has a thick coat of soft hair. Although the hair looks white, it is actually transparent. Sunlight passes through the transparent hair to the animal's skin. The sunlight warms the skin, and the thick hair holds the heat in. After about three weeks, the pup grows coarse gray hair that replaces the soft birth coat. During these first weeks, the pup drinks its mother's milk and gains great amounts of weight. When the pup's new coat grows in, the mother leaves the pup and swims north for the summer months. The pup remains with other pups on the ice. It lives off its supply of blubber. When

Rising through a hole in the ice, a harp seal sniffs her pup (above) off the coast of Quebec, in Canada. A female seal can tell her own pup from hundreds of others on the ice by its scent and its cries. Another harp seal guards her pup (left). The pups do not enter the cold water until they have developed a layer of blubber beneath the skin.

A snowy owl feeds her chicks in her nest on the ground (above). When hatched, the chicks were white. They matched the snow around them. As the snow melted, the chicks grew grayish feathers, blending with the snow-free ground. Enemies often don't spot chicks that match their surroundings.

the ice melts a week or two later, the pup enters the water and swims north with the other young seals.

Various kinds of polar animals live on the tundra, far from the waters of the polar bear and the seal. Many birds visit the tundra in the summer to nest and to raise young. They leave before the long arctic winter sets in. Few kinds of animals stay active on the tundra year round. Among those that do are arctic foxes and small creatures called collared lemmings. These permanent residents change their coats with the seasons. In the summer, their colors tend to match the ground and plants. In the winter, white hair disguises the animals on the snow.

The matching of an animal's color or shape to its surroundings is called camouflage (KAM-uh-flazh). Camouflage helps predators—animals that hunt other animals for food. It also helps prey—the animals that are hunted for food. Predators, such as arctic foxes and weasels, can approach their prey while camouflaged on the ground or on the snow around them. At the same time, prey, such as collared lemmings, may hide themselves among plants

FRED BRUEMMER

Willow ptarmigan (TAR-mih-gun) chicks huddle on the ground (above). The pattern of their soft down feathers helps hide them until they can fly.

STEPHEN J. KRASEMANN/DRK PHOTO

WAYNE LANKINEN

In the fall, a willow ptarmigan begins to molt (left). It sheds its brown summer feathers for winter white. This bird lives on the ground among the willow thickets that grow in much of the lower Arctic. In winter, it roosts on soft snow.

Snow-white feathers help a rock ptarmigan blend with the snow (above). In winter, the ptarmigan grows feather coverings on its toes (right). Like snowshoes, the feathers help the bird walk on top of snow.

An arctic fox has a brown-and-white summer coat of short hair (above). In winter, the fox grows a white—and longer—coat (right). Changing coats with the changing seasons helps the fox approach prey without being spotted. The thick coat of the arctic fox also helps it keep warm at temperatures that may dip as low as minus 50°F (−46°C). Curled up, the fox often warms its nose with its tail.

The collared lemming (left) uses its sharp claws to dig burrows. Its brown summer coat helps hide it on the tundra from such enemies as arctic foxes. The tundra is the treeless land of the far north. In winter, the lemming grows a white coat (below). It is the only one of the rodents—animals such as mice and squirrels—that grows a white winter coat. The lemming's claws grow larger in winter. They help the animal dig through snow to reach plants.

Arctic hares gather in summer on bare ground in far northern Canada. At this time of year, their coats stand out against the earth. The hares depend on speed to escape foxes and wolves. On winter snow, the hares often go unseen by enemies.

or on snow, well camouflaged against predators.

Like several of their neighbors, arctic hares in many parts of the far north change color from season to season. However, not all arctic hares change color. Those that live farthest north, where summers are shortest, stay white year round. These permanently white hares often gather in large groups on the open tundra. In winter, their white fur grows thicker and longer than in summer.

The arctic hare has smaller ears than other kinds of hares. Small ears lose less body heat than large ears do because they expose less skin to the cold. Small ears help the hare save heat in winter.

The arctic hare feeds on grasses, and the twigs and roots of willows. It uses the claws on its large front feet to dig through crusted snow to find food. For shelter in winter, the hare sometimes digs itself a cave in a packed snowdrift. The snow traps a layer of air around the animal. The trapped air acts as a blanket, keeping out the cold.

An arctic hare stands on trampled snow. To sit on snow, the hare rests most of its weight on the large pads of its hind feet. The thick hair of the pads protects the animal from the cold. In winter, the hare flattens its ears and huddles into a ball for warmth.

Animals on the Hoof

Large, hoofed creatures make their homes in the Arctic, too. Like their smaller neighbors, the hoofed animals have adaptations that equip them for survival in this often frozen land.

Herds of sturdy musk-oxen graze all year long in the high Arctic. This area includes the part of the tundra that borders the arctic seas. Plant life is scarce. Icy winter winds sweep the high Arctic.

Eskimos call musk-oxen "the animals with skin like a beard" because of their long hair. The heavy hair hangs all over the animals, even around their

muzzles. It may grow as long as 2 feet (2/3 m). The hair protects the musk-oxen from the coldest winds. A thick layer of fine, soft wool grows underneath the long, coarse hair. The undercoat provides extra warmth in winter.

Musk-oxen feed on grasses and willows. Their hooves have sharp rims that provide firm footing on snowy slopes in winter. The rims also prove useful for scraping away crusts of snow and for digging down to reach food underneath.

Caribou, members of the deer family, live in

© THOR LARSEN

Facing danger head-on, musk-oxen form a tight circle (left). Their sharp horns point outward. All of the musk-oxen in the herd form such a circle of defense when a wolf or other predator begins circling them.

Shaggy coats brushing the snow, musk-oxen dig down to grasses in Greenland (below). A thick coat of fine wool under their long hair keeps out the cold.

17

herds larger than those of musk-oxen. Musk-oxen may live in groups of as many as 60 animals. Caribou sometimes travel in groups of several thousand. In these large herds, the caribou migrate across the tundra, keeping almost constantly on the move. In North America, caribou live in parts of Canada and Alaska. Some are found in parts of Greenland. In the northern parts of Asia and Europe where these deer live, they are called reindeer.

Most caribou in North America migrate every year between the northern tundra and the forests to the south. After a summer of grazing on the tundra, the caribou start south. The tundra they leave behind will be buried under crusted snow. Harsh winter winds will blow across that open landscape.

The journey of the caribou continues day and night across bare ground, snow, and rivers. In winter, the outer edges of the animals' hooves grow longer, providing a grip on snow and ice. The soft pads inside the horny hooves shrink. Hair covers the pads, protecting them from rough ice.

When the caribou reach the forests, the trees provide food, and cover from the winds. Among the trees, the snow remains soft, making it easier than on the tundra for the caribou to dig down to the plants they eat off the ground.

In spring, the caribou herds leave the forests and return north to the tundra. Females bear their young on the way. During the migration, the caribou may travel more than 400 miles (644 km).

On a slope in northern Alaska, a young caribou trails its mother (left). A newborn caribou can stand up just minutes after its birth. Within a few hours, it can walk and keep up with its mother. Some caribou herds number in the thousands. Every year, the herds migrate between summer and winter feeding grounds. The migrations often cover hundreds of miles. Like all other kinds of deer, caribou grow antlers—and shed them—every year. Among the other deer, however, only the males grow antlers. Among caribou, females grow them, too.

A herd of caribou (left) swims a river in Canada's Yukon Territory during the fall migration. The caribou have grown thick winter coats. The hairs are hollow and hold air that helps insulate the animals against the cold. These animals are called caribou in North America and in Greenland. In Europe and Asia, they are known as reindeer.

Pawing through the snow (right), a caribou uncovers plants called lichens (LIE-kuns). Lichens grow extremely slowly. Since caribou depend on these plants for food, the herds must stay on the move to find enough to eat.

A caribou's foot (right) serves the animal well all year long. Each foot has four hoofed toes, two large and two small. The large toes spread apart on soft ground and on snow. They keep the caribou from sinking in. Dewclaws, the small toes on the back of the foot, help support the caribou only on very soft surfaces. Sharp outer edges of the hooves on the large toes provide a grip on ice.

Way Down South

If you look for penguins north of the Equator, you may find them, but just in zoos. Penguins in the wild live only south of the Equator. Seven kinds live on the ice and in the cold seas of the Antarctic.

Penguins cannot fly. However, they do use their wings—as flippers underwater. Flapping along, they can propel themselves through water as fast as 25 miles an hour (40 km/h)—faster than any other water birds. Penguins can dive hundreds of feet deep in search of food. They hunt for fish, squids, and shrimplike animals called krill.

Penguins have small, stiff feathers. The feathers overlap and grow close together. As many as 300 grow in an area as small as a postage stamp. The feathers keep the birds' bodies dry. Fluffy down

Splash! Adélie (uh-DAY-lee) penguins plunge into Antarctic waters. Feathers that grow close together and overlap keep the penguins' bodies dry. Staying dry helps the birds keep warm in the water.

feathers under the waterproof coats help keep the penguins warm. Penguins produce oil in a gland near the tail. Using their bills and the edges of their wings, they put a thin film of this oil on their feathers. This helps keep the feathers waterproof.

Most kinds of penguins breed and raise young on land. As many as a million penguins may gather at a single rookery, or breeding ground.

Adélie (uh-DAY-lee) penguins build nests of pebbles on the ground. The female usually lays two eggs. Both parents take turns sitting on the nest and keeping the eggs warm.

Emperor penguins do not build nests. They lay their eggs directly on the sea ice. After laying a single egg, the female goes off to feed at sea. Her mate immediately scoops the egg onto his feet and covers it with a feathered fold of belly skin. There, he keeps it warm until it hatches about two months later. During that time, the male eats nothing. He lives off fat stored in his body. He tends the egg through the coldest part of the winter. Winds may howl at 100 miles an hour (161 km/h). Temperatures may drop to 70° below zero Fahrenheit (–57°C). The males turn their backs to the wind, huddling to help each other keep warm.

The emperor penguin's feet have no blubber or feathers. But the bird avoids losing too much heat through its feet. Frequently, the emperor penguin leans back on its feet, props itself with its tail, and lifts its toes off the ice. Scientists believe this

Rising to turn its egg, a nesting Adélie penguin reveals a patch of bare skin on its belly (left). Called the brood patch, this skin is crisscrossed with blood vessels. Heat from the adult penguin's blood helps keep the egg warm in the nest of pebbles.

A down-covered Adélie chick lifts its beak to its parent, begging for a meal (above). The adult bird has a mass of partially digested food in its throat. When the adult opens its mouth, the hungry chick will stick its head inside to gobble the food. Penguin parents feed only their own chicks. Parents returning with food from the sea recognize their chicks by their cries.

Like parent, like chick. Sitting on ice in the Antarctic, an emperor penguin and its chick lift up their toes (below). Scientists believe this behavior helps the penguins avoid losing too much body heat through their feet during long periods on the ice.

An emperor penguin chick peers from its perch atop a parent's feet (right). The emperor doesn't build a nest. The female lays an egg and the parents raise the young on the sea ice. To keep the egg warm, the male places it on his feet. He shelters it with a feathered fold of belly skin. After the egg hatches, the parents take turns warming the chick by holding it on their feet. Fully grown, an emperor stands about 3 feet (1 m) tall, larger than any other penguin.

habit helps it avoid the cold. Also, the penguin's blood circulates in a special way. Blood in the feet cools quickly. If the cooler blood from the feet were to flow back into the central part of the body—the body core—it would chill the penguin. But as the cooled blood flows toward the body core, it passes next to warmer blood entering the feet. Thus, the warmer blood heats the cooler blood before it flows back into the body core.

Penguins face danger both above and below the water. Young penguins are easy prey on land and on ice. Gulls and large birds called skuas (SKEW-uhs) prey on them. In the water, leopard seals and killer whales wait near penguin rookeries. They catch the penguins as the birds enter the water. Sometimes adult penguins can escape leopard seals and killer whales by swimming at full speed, then leaping out of the water onto the ice.

FRANK S. TODD, SEA WORLD, INC.

Surfacing, a leopard seal surprises an Adélie penguin (above). The penguin flaps and calls, warning other penguins. Leopard seals often hunt penguins by waiting for them at the edge of the ice.

On floating ice, a leopard seal rests after a meal. This seal gets its name from the spots on its coat. The leopard seal has pointed teeth suited for grasping and tearing flesh. Besides preying on penguins, the leopard seal catches fish, squids, and other kinds of seals and birds.

D E S E R T S

CLEM HAAGNER/BRUCE COLEMAN INC.

Camels move across hot sand on the Kalahari Desert, in southern Africa. Coats of thick woolly hair protect their skin from the direct rays of the blazing sun. Camels can live for several days without drinking water.

The desert: By day, it broils under the glaring sun. By night, it becomes cool. What little rain falls on the desert can come in a single downpour. The water quickly evaporates or soaks into the ground. Then for months, no rain may fall.

Deserts are the earth's driest lands. The average desert rainfall is less than 10 inches (25 cm) a year. Some deserts receive an average of only half an inch (1 cm) a year. Only the hardiest plants, such as cactuses, can grow in such a land.

The sun heats up some deserts well over 100°F (38°C) during the day. Hours later, at night, you might feel chilled there. These great temperature changes occur because desert air is so dry. Unlike more humid regions, deserts have no layer of moist air that shields them from the sun's rays and that holds in heat at night. Desert-dwelling animals must avoid or withstand the extremes of heat and cold. They must survive in areas that contain little water.

Deserts have one thing in common: dryness. Most are hot by day. Some are cold. Orange areas show hot deserts (above). Gold areas show cold deserts. In this chapter, you'll read only about hot deserts.

Perched cautiously on the longest spines of a cactus, a Harris's antelope ground squirrel eyes the cactus fruit (right). The squirrel stays active in midday heat in the Arizona desert. Its body temperature can rise a few degrees without harm to the animal.

26

JEN AND DES BARTLETT (OPPOSITE)

Desert Traveler

The Arabian, or one-humped, camel lives in herds on the deserts of Africa and Asia. Hot, dry winds blow across the sandy lands. In many areas, no plants grow as far as the eye can see.

Living on the desert, camels often must travel long distances without eating or drinking. They can travel more than 600 miles (966 km) without a sip of water. They feed on desert plants that provide much of the moisture they need. Many desert plants have thorns. Camels' mouths, however, are tough enough to manage even the thorniest plants.

Although many people believe that camels store water in their humps, the animals don't. Camels' humps are storage areas for fat. Camels do have special ways of preserving body moisture, however. They do not begin to sweat until their temperature

rises several degrees above normal. They eliminate only small amounts of urine, and they recapture most of the moisture in their breath before the air leaves their noses. Surfaces inside their noses absorb moisture from the air the camels breathe out.

When camels reach water, they may drink great quantities—until their bellies bulge. A camel may drink as much as 30 gallons (114 L) at one time.

In a desert in Saudi Arabia (above), camels plod through a driving sandstorm. A camel's head (left) has several features that protect the animal from blowing sand. The nostrils can squeeze into narrow slits that don't let sand through. Long, thick eyelashes help filter out blowing sand. The camel's eyelids let light through, allowing the camel to walk during a sandstorm with its eyes shut. Thick hair grows in the ears, keeping sand out.

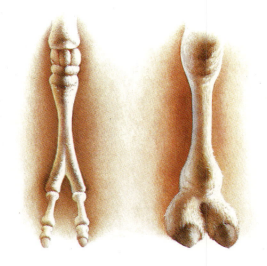

Wide foot pads help a camel walk on loose, shifting sand. The bones of the camel's two toes (above, left) are widely separated. A broad foot pad underneath connects the two toes (above, right). When the camel walks, the cushionlike pad spreads out across the sand. This keeps the animal from sinking in.

29

In southern California, a fringe-toed lizard dashes across desert sand (above). The lizard has fringes of flat scales on its hind feet. They help the animal run on sand. They also help it wriggle rapidly under sand to flee rattlesnakes and other enemies.

A desert tortoise takes a bite of an Arizona desert plant (below). The tortoise gets most of the water it needs from the plants it eats. The tortoise has a bladder, or sac, in its body that stores water.

An American Desert

Deserts cover much of Mexico and the southwestern United States. One of the most colorful deserts, the Sonoran, stretches from southeastern California across southern Arizona and into Mexico. Bright flowers appear among the white, red, and tan sands after early spring rain showers. Cactuses thrive on the desert year round. Some of the cactuses found on the Sonoran Desert grow nowhere else. Many kinds of animals find homes in this environment. All of the animals on this and the next five pages may be found in the Sonoran Desert.

One resident, the desert tortoise, has thick, tough skin on its neck and legs. This skin helps protect the tortoise from thorns—and from losing too much moisture in the sun's heat. The tortoise seldom needs to drink. It obtains moisture from the plants it eats. The tortoise stores some of this moisture in a large bladder, or sac, in its body. During dry periods, it can live on the stored moisture. In the hottest hours, it burrows underground.

Many desert animals stay out of the sun during

Nibbling leaves in the shadows of a desert bush, a black-tailed jackrabbit avoids the sun. Its huge ears help the animal cool off. Heat escapes to the air from blood vessels near the surface of the skin of the jackrabbit's ears.

the midday heat. Snakes, insects, spiders, and most small rodents, in addition to tortoises, hide underground in cool burrows. Other animals, such as coyotes and jackrabbits, rest in the shade of rocks and plants. All these animals usually feed during the night, or in the cool evening and morning hours.

Some desert creatures remain active in daylight. One kind of movement you might see would be that of a lizard rushing across the sand. The fringe-toed lizard lives in the sandy parts of the desert. It feeds on insects. The light color of its body helps it blend with the sand and hide from predators, such as birds. To escape danger, the lizard can run quickly across the dry desert surface. Scales on its hind feet give the lizard a grip on the ground, even though the surface is soft sand. The lizard can also dive into the sand and bury itself in just seconds. Its fringed toes help it wriggle and burrow so

fast that it seems actually to "swim" through the sand. In the sand, the lizard can close its ears with small flaps of skin. It can squeeze its nostrils almost shut. An extra, clear eyelid protects each eye. The lizard's lower jaw fits tightly into its upper jaw, keeping sand out of the mouth.

Huge, fingerlike cactuses tower above the lizard's sandy home on the Sonoran Desert. These cactuses, called saguaros (suh-WAHR-ohz), grow in no other desert. A saguaro can grow as high as a five-story building. It may live as long as 200 years.

Saguaro cactuses provide food and shelter for many desert animals. Birds, bats, and moths feed on nectar from the cactus flowers. Other animals eat the plant's pulpy red fruit when it falls to the ground. For some desert creatures, the saguaro serves as a house. Desert woodpeckers chisel out new nesting holes each year. The holes reach deep

An elf owl peers from inside a tall saguaro (suh-WAHR-oh) cactus (left). The owl sleeps by day inside a hole in the plant. Woodpeckers called northern flickers (below) drill such holes for nests. Here, a flicker perches by a nest next to her mate. After the woodpeckers leave, the owls often move in.

With food for its young, a cactus wren stands near its nest in a cholla (CHOY-uh) cactus (above). The cactus spines help protect the nest from predators.

into the cactus like pockets. The thick cactus walls protect the nesting birds from the desert heat. The nests provide safety from most predators because the cactus is so tall and is covered by sharp spines. After the woodpeckers raise their young and leave their nests, other creatures, such as elf owls, move in. The abandoned nests provide cool resting places during the day for the new occupants.

Another kind of cactus, the cholla (CHOY-uh), provides protection for other animals. The cholla grows in small sections, each covered with needle-sharp spines. The spiny sections are useful to the wood rat. It piles them for protection around its nest on the ground. The cactus wren and the road-runner both nest among the cactus branches. The spines protect the birds' nests as barbed wire would.

The roadrunner, one of the swiftest desert hunters, uses its long tail and its wings for balance as it races and zigzags over the ground after prey. The roadrunner moves so fast it can kill a rattlesnake be-fore the snake strikes. The bird circles the snake. Then it rushes in, grabbing at the snake with its beak. The roadrunner was named for its habit of racing across roads in front of moving vehicles.

A roadrunner races across a California desert (above). To chase after prey or to flee enemies, the roadrunner usually runs instead of flying. It speeds along as fast as 20 miles an hour (32 km/h). Zigzagging, it catches lizards and other prey.

Fluffing up its outer feathers (left), a young roadrunner exposes a dark patch of skin and down feathers on its back. The dark area helps the bird warm up after a cold night. The roadrunner points the patch toward the sun. The dark skin and down absorb the sun's heat. When the bird has warmed up, it lowers its feathers over the patch.

Salt collects around a nostril in a roadrunner's beak (left). A gland near the eye extracted the salt from the bird's blood and deposited the salt at the nostril. Normally, the bird gets rid of salt from its blood through its kidneys. The salt is eliminated in urine. But when water is scarce, the bird can extract salt from its blood with its nasal gland. The gland helps the roadrunner eliminate salt while losing less fluid than it would by using its kidneys.

Dwellers in Africa's Namib Desert

One of the most unusual deserts in the world, the Namib, lies along the west coast of southern Africa. There, blowing wind piles sand into towering dunes. The largest dunes rise 1,000 feet (305 m) above the dune valleys. Although the desert lies near the sea, the moist sea air does not provide the desert with rain. This is because cold ocean currents chill the sea air. Since cold air does not rise, the chilled sea air cannot form rain clouds that might blow inland. As a result, parts of the Namib get less than an inch (2½ cm) of rain a year. Some areas of the desert get no rain for years.

In a desert so dry, so sandy, and with so few plants, it might seem unlikely that animals would be able to survive. Yet more kinds of animals live in the sand dunes of the Namib than in the sand dunes of all other deserts of the world combined.

Even though it rarely rains in the Namib, the desert does get a supply of moisture. The moist sea air often forms into thick clouds of fog. The fog sometimes blows inland over the desert. At ground level, the moisture from the fog becomes available to living creatures. Many animals that live on the Namib have ways of gathering this moisture and using it for their survival.

One kind of tenebrionid (tuh-NEB-ree-uh-nud)

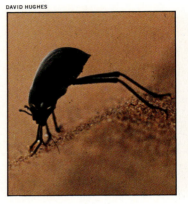

On a sand dune in the Namib, a tenebrionid (tuh-NEB-ree-uh-nud) beetle sips a drop of water (far left). To get water, the beetle raises its back end into a foggy wind. Droplets collect on its body and roll down to its mouth. After drinking, the beetle digs into the sand (left) to avoid birds and other predators.

Droplets from morning fog collect on the body of a web-footed gecko (right). The gecko will lick the moisture off its head, then burrow deep into the sand. Burrowing keeps it cool during the day. Webbed feet help it dig. Like other desert predators, the gecko gets most of its moisture from the body fluids of its prey.

A sidewinding viper buries itself in the sand, showing little more than its eyes (left). Hidden this way, the snake waits for lizards and other prey to come near. Then, striking quickly, it kills its prey with a poisonous bite. Like the gecko, the sidewinding viper makes use of morning fog. It licks collected water droplets off its own body (below) before the day heats up and the droplets evaporate.

Lifting its tail and feet off the desert sand keeps a sand-diving lizard (above) from becoming too hot. The lizard eats insects and seeds. To flee a bird or *other predator, the lizard plows headfirst into the sand with its shovel-like snout. Then it twists its entire body under the surface.*

A sand-diving lizard peers from a sandy hiding place (above). To avoid the heat of the midday sun, it will dig deeper, to where the sand is cooler.

beetle drinks the moisture of the fog after it collects in droplets on its body. To collect water from the fog, another kind of beetle, the button beetle, makes a narrow trench in the sand. As the fog blows across this trench, moisture collects on the raised edges. The beetle waits for the moisture to collect. Then it moves back along the edges of the trench and sucks the water from the sand.

Some beetles in parts of the Namib are active only during the day. They search the sand for bits of leaves and seeds blown from dune valleys where plants grow. At night, they burrow into the sand. There, the sun-warmed sand will keep them warmer than they would be in the cold night air.

Many animals cannot stand the heat of the desert air during the day. By day, they stay underground in burrows, which remain cooler than the

By day, the dune cricket (left) usually avoids desert heat by burying itself beneath the surface. Above ground, the dry desert air would cause the cricket's body to lose too much moisture. Underground, the air is moist. The cricket comes out to feed at night, when the air is cooler. It eats bits of seeds and leaves blown near it by the wind.

air outside. Above ground, the day and night temperatures vary enormously. But below the surface, the temperature differences between day and night are far less extreme.

Animals that are active mainly at night are called nocturnal. Nocturnal animals, such as Namib gerbils, avoid the heat of the day and also avoid losing precious moisture. The air in burrows underground contains much more moisture than does the air above the ground. Animals in burrows lose less moisture to the air around them than they would in the dry air above the ground.

In a land where water is so scarce, the Namib gerbil has a special way of managing. It doesn't need to drink at all. The Namib gerbil cannot move long distances in search of water holes or moist grasses. It would rapidly become overheated. Instead, it gathers its food—dry grasses, seeds, and insects—near its burrow in the coolness of the night. It returns with its food to eat it in the burrow. From this food, the gerbil gets the small amount of water

Much enlarged, a dune cricket's foot shows tiny bristly spurs. The bristles spread out on the sand, helping the cricket gain a foothold so that it can hop.

Curled up in its burrow (right), a spider called a dancing white lady holds its prey, a dune cricket. The spider weaves sand into its sticky web over the burrow entrance. The web helps hide the entrance from predators. At night, the spider leaves its burrow and hunts insects on the desert surface.

A round hole in the sand (above) marks the entrance to a gerbil burrow. Gerbils usually dig burrows under clumps of dune grass. The roots of the grass help hold the sand together.

Nestled together, two gerbils sleep in their burrow (below). During the day, the gerbils remain underground, avoiding the scorching heat. At night, the animals search the desert outside their burrows for grasses, seeds, insects, and roots to eat.

it needs. The animal has a way of preserving as much of that water as possible. The gerbil's efficient kidneys concentrate its urine. The gerbil thus eliminates little water with its waste. (Although related, the Namib gerbil is not the same kind of gerbil commonly kept as a pet.)

Another Namib animal you might find active at night is a spider known as the dancing white lady. It gets its name from the way it "dances" on its long legs when threatened. The display may serve to frighten off a predator, such as a golden mole. To avoid a predator, the spider exits in a hurry. It folds up its legs and cartwheels quickly down a slope. This method of escape works well in the Namib, since the desert has so many steep sand dunes.

Many animals of the Namib use camouflage as an important tool for survival. The desert has few plants that provide hiding places. Many Namib animals have reddish or rusty coloring. This helps them blend with the color of the sand. As in the Arctic, both predators and prey benefit from matching their environment. The hunters, such as snakes, are hard for the hunted to spot. Likewise, the hunted, such as lizards, are often difficult for the hunters to find.

A snake called the sidewinding viper is well adapted to hide as it hunts. Its color closely resembles the color of the sand. The snake's eyes and nostrils lie almost on top of its head. This allows the snake to bury itself almost completely in the sand as it watches for prey. Any part of the snake that shows almost exactly matches the surface of the desert.

Whiskers twitching, a bright-eyed gerbil steps from its burrow. The gerbil has a keen sense of hearing. This often helps it escape from predators. The gerbil can hear even the faintest rustle of an approaching snake at night.

Animal Look-alikes and Act-alikes

Related kinds of animals often live far apart in the world. Take, for example, camels and vicuñas. They have common ancestors. But camels live on deserts of Africa and Asia. Vicuñas live in the Andes, mountains in South America. Although they are related, camels and vicuñas have different habits, coats, colors, shapes, and diets. The camel and the vicuña have another difference: They live in different biomes.

Other distantly related animals live in separate parts of the world, too. But sometimes, they live in very much the same kind of biome. When that happens, the two kinds of animals often develop similar forms and habits over a long period of time. The challenges to survival are similar in the deserts of Africa, Asia, and North America. Several kinds of desert animals around the world have developed similar ways of living with these

ANIMALS ANIMALS/OSF-J.A.L. COOKE

The jerboa (left) and the kangaroo rat (below) look and act much alike, but they are only distantly related. The jerboa lives in Africa and Asia. The kangaroo rat lives in North America. The two have developed similar ways in similar desert homes, however. To flee enemies, both take extra-long hops on powerful rear legs. Special lights and equipment were used to record the kangaroo rat's jumping motion.

N.G.S. PHOTOGRAPHER BRUCE DALE (BELOW)

Two distantly related snakes have developed the same method of moving across desert sand. The sidewinder rattlesnake (left) lives in southwestern North America. The sidewinding viper (above) lives in Africa's Namib Desert. To move along, both snakes loop their bodies sideways. They get a grip on the loose sand by pushing down into it with the looped parts of their long bodies.

challenges. On safari in widely separated deserts, you might well find similar animals.

Water shortage is one of the biggest problems desert animals face. Some animals, such as the tenebrionid beetle, have unusual ways of gathering water. Some, such as the camel, can go for days without drinking. Others—desert frogs and toads—have ways of holding in their moisture and waiting long periods until water again becomes available.

Frogs and toads absorb moisture and lose it through their skin. You might think that they would dry out quickly in the desert air. They would, if they stayed active year round. But desert frogs in Australia and desert toads in South America have ways of surviving in their dry environments.

After the brief summer rains, desert toads burrow into mud. There, they become dormant, or inactive. This is called aestivation (es-tuh-VAY-shun). In many ways, aestivation is like the hibernation of animals during cold winter months. The heart rate slows down, and the animal uses little energy. Unlike hibernation, however, aestivation takes place in

A burrowing frog of Australia (above) sleeps in a mud chamber. It digs the chamber and remains buried there for months at a time during the desert dry season. A thin, dry layer of dead skin surrounds the frog, holding in moisture. When rain falls, the frog will eat the covering and dig its way out.

hot or dry periods. Wrapped in protective coverings of dead skin, the toads remain underground until the next rainy season. In times of severe drought, aestivation may last several years.

Several kinds of animals can live a lifetime without drinking a swallow of water. Like the Namib gerbil, the kangaroo rat of North America and the jerboa of Africa and Asia never need to drink. They get enough moisture from their food, and they eliminate little water in their waste.

The kangaroo rat and the jerboa are alike in other ways. They have similar feet and legs. Their long hind legs help them jump to escape enemies. The two animals can spring straight off the ground to avoid the teeth or claws of foxes, snakes, or other enemies. They can also leap long distances while fleeing predators. The kangaroo rat and the jerboa have furry soles on their hind feet. These help both creatures get a grip on the sand as they jump.

Some desert insects have similar features that are useful for traveling over sand. The sand cricket of North America has bristly spurs on its feet. They help it leap on loose sand just as the feet of the dune cricket of Africa help it.

At first glance, the North American kit fox and the fennec of Africa and the Middle East look much alike, almost as if they were the same animal. The kit fox, however, grows a bit larger—about the size

A South American desert toad (above) comes out from a long period underground. Like the desert frog of Australia, this toad buries itself through the dry season. It rests in a burrow for most of the year. Underground, the toad produces a covering of dead skin that keeps its body from drying out.

Summer rain signaled a South American desert toad to surface and shed its wrapping (right). At the surface, it will feed and mate. Brief but heavy rain forms temporary pools. Toads breed and lay their eggs in the pools. The young toads develop before the pools dry up. Then the young bury themselves in mud and wait for the next year's rain.

N.G.S. PHOTOGRAPHER BRUCE DALE (BOTH)

of a house cat. Both foxes have furry, sand-colored coats. The coats help them blend with the color of the desert and keep them warm on cold nights.

The most obvious similarity between the two desert foxes is their ears. Both have large ears compared with body size. Fennecs have the largest ears of any kind of fox. They may grow as long as 6 inches (15 cm). The huge ears help both kinds of foxes hear insects, rodents, lizards, and other prey. The large size of the ears helps the foxes in another way. On hot days, the ears act as radiators, giving off heat. Blood vessels flow through the foxes' thin ears. The blood passes heat to the air. This heat loss helps cool off the foxes.

Desert animals live in areas of extreme dryness, heat, and cold. People often think of deserts as empty, barren places where little life survives. As you have seen, however, a great many animals not only live on the desert—they thrive there. Many of them have adapted so well that it is unlikely that they could live anywhere else.

A desert kit fox of North America (above) closely resembles fennecs of Africa and the Middle East (right). Both have developed in similar desert conditions, although the foxes are not closely related. Large ears help them hear the slightest noises from small prey, such as insects and rodents.

RAIN FORESTS

LOREN MCINTYRE

From the air, the rain forest looks like a deep tangle of greenery (above). Here, birds called macaws add splashes of color. The rain forest supports more kinds of plants and animals than any other place on earth.

The rain forest is a lush, green world. Throughout the year the climate stays about the same: hot and steamy. For much of the year, rain falls every day or two. It often comes in heavy downpours. The warm, wet climate makes the rain forest a giant greenhouse. Trees and plants of many different kinds bloom year round. Giant trees rise as high as 20-story buildings. Flowers and ferns grow on tree limbs, and vines twist around the trunks. On the shady floor of the forest, few green plants grow. Fungus thrives on decaying plant matter.

The trees and other plants provide food and living space for a wide variety of animals. Animals live at different levels in the rain forest. Some live in the tops of the tallest trees. Many live among the thick branches. Some are found along the tree trunks. Others spend their lives on or under the forest floor. Animals at each level have their own ways of moving about and finding food.

Tropical rain forests, shaded in green (above), circle the earth north and south of the Equator. South America has the world's largest rain forest.

In the rain forest of Sumatra, a large island of Indonesia, a young orangutan dangles in the sunny treetops (right). Orangutans spend most of their time high in the trees. Grasping with hands and feet, they swing from branch to branch.

In the middle of a long leap, a squirrel monkey reaches for a branch. Her baby rides piggyback, clutching its mother's hair. Squirrel monkeys live high off the ground in the rain forests of Central and South America. They travel through the treetops by climbing and leaping among the branches. Squirrel monkeys travel in large groups, called troops, with as many as 50 members.

Treetop Life

Insects and birds dart here and there among the tallest trees in the rain forest. The crowns of these trees make up the part of the forest called the emergent layer. The crowns poke through the thick layer of branches, leaves, and vines that surround them.

The green layer below the tops of the tallest trees is actually the top of the next rain forest layer, the canopy. The sun shines bright and hot on the roof of the canopy. When rain clouds roll in, they turn the canopy into a darkened, dripping world. A rich supply of fruit, leaves, and nuts grows year round among the tangle of the canopy branches. In this green and humid world, animals fly, glide, leap, and climb. They gather food, hunt, hide, sleep, and raise young among the branches and vines. Many seldom descend to the ground. They have special adaptations that help them live in trees.

One way of getting around in the canopy is a combination of leaping, swinging, and jumping. Various kinds of rain forest monkeys are experts at this. They live as high as 100 feet (30 m) above the ground. Strong arms and legs make them well suited to moving among the branches.

Some monkeys have long tails that can grasp branches and other objects. Called prehensile (pre-HEN-sul) tails, they are useful adaptations for animals that live in natural jungle gyms. The spider monkey, one of the largest rain forest monkeys,

A spider monkey in Mexico dangles by its tail (right). The grasping tail helps the monkey swing among the branches. A bare patch of skin near the end of the tail improves the monkey's grip. The hands are well adapted for swinging. Each hand has four long fingers, but no thumb. The fingers hook around branches as the monkey swings.

The rain forest consists of several layers of plant life (below). Each is home to many kinds of animals. In the emergent layer, the crowns of the tallest trees tower above their neighbors. Below, in the canopy, branches, leaves, and vines grow tangled in a thick mass. Small bushes and young trees grow in the understory, with plenty of space between them. Almost no direct sunlight reaches the damp forest floor, where few plants grow.

Emergent layer

Canopy

Understory

Floor

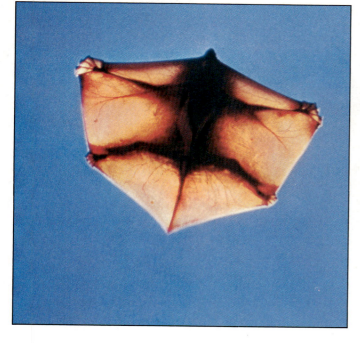

A blue-and-yellow macaw (below) uses its beak for help in climbing. It anchors the upper part of its beak on the bark, then steps up the branch. The macaw, of Central and South America, also uses its beak to crack open seeds and hard nuts. The bird takes out the nutmeats with its thick, fleshy tongue.

Hanging onto a branch, a flying lemur, or colugo (kuh-LOO-go), cradles her young in loose folds of skin (left). The folds of skin extend along her sides from the neck to the tail. The colugo climbs well, but it has an even faster way of moving from tree to tree: It glides. When it leaps from one tree to another, it spreads its limbs wide (above). The stretched folds of skin become tight flaps with which the animal glides through the air. The colugo lives in rain forests of Southeast Asia.

lives in Central and South America. Its prehensile tail is longer than the rest of its body. A spider monkey uses the end of its tail as an extra hand. It can pick up fruit and nuts with the tail, and can use it to grasp and swing from branches.

The monkeys of the canopy have some colorful neighbors. Many kinds of brilliantly colored birds live among the thick tangle of branches and leaves. Although birds can simply flutter from one forest level to another, most don't. Like so many of the nonflying creatures of the rain forest, birds generally are adapted best to one forest level.

Macaws and other kinds of parrots have hard, heavy beaks that help them feed on fruit and nuts in

...ts on a branch munching a leaf
...'s most of its life hanging
...d claws. It lives in the
...America. The
...ccasionally.

...ain forest
...ly drag
...inging

two wide flaps of skin along its sides. The colugo steers by moving its legs and tail. It often covers 200 feet (61 m) in a single glide. A young colugo glides with its mother, clinging to the fur of her belly.

The rain forest has other gliders. Lizards in the forests of Southeast Asia have huge flaps of skin on their sides. The lizards, called flying dragons, stretch out their flaps by extending several ribs on each side. Some snakes of Southeast Asia are also gliders. They pull in their bellies and push down their sides until they resemble flattened fire hoses. In this shape, the snakes sail from branch to branch, or to the ground, chasing prey or fleeing enemies. Tropical frogs of Southeast Asia can glide as far as 40 feet (12 m). These frogs spread their fingers and toes wide. Skin between the fingers and toes forms thin pads. The pads help the frogs stay airborne.

Some canopy animals move slowly. In the rain forests of Central and South America, the sloth proceeds at a snail's pace—when it moves at all. The sloth usually just hangs upside down from a tree branch by its long, curved claws. Sleeping as much as 15 hours a day in that position, it also eats, moves around, and even gives birth upside down.

A sloth's hair grows from its belly toward its

Tiny plants called algae (AL-gee) turned the hair of a three-toed sloth greenish (right). The algae grow in grooves in the sloth's hairs. Hanging in the trees motionless and wearing a green coat makes the sloth almost invisible to eagles and other enemies.

backbone. The direction of the hair helps make rainwater run off the sloth's body as the animal hangs from all fours.

One kind of sloth—the three-toed, shown on pages 54 and 55—has nine neck bones. That's two more than mice, monkeys, horses, and even giraffes have. The extra neckbones allow this sloth to turn its head in almost every direction. Hanging from a branch, the animal can twist its head to browse on leaves around it without moving the rest of its body.

The sloth's extreme slowness in everything it does allows it to survive on little energy. You'd think that its slow-motion habits would make it easy prey for eagles and hunting cats. But in the trees, the sloth moves so seldom—and so slowly—that enemies often overlook it.

Like the sloth, the slow loris, of Southeast Asia, travels in slow motion wherever it goes. This might seem an unlikely way to move for an animal that eats lizards, insects, and other fast-moving small animals. But the slow loris takes advantage of its slowness. Instead of chasing prey, it sneaks up on its targets. It approaches so slowly that prey animals seldom notice it coming.

Using its twiglike fingers, an aye-aye (left) digs for larvae, or insect young. The aye-aye uses its sharp hearing to detect larvae under the bark. Then it bites off the bark with chisel-like front teeth. It uses its long middle finger, shown in the enlarged view, to spear the larvae. Then it eats them. This rare animal lives in Madagascar, an island nation off the coast of Africa.

Extra-strong hands and feet help a slow loris cling to a thin branch (left). This animal lives in rain forests in much of Southeast Asia. The slow loris creeps so slowly toward lizards and other prey that they often don't notice it approaching. When the slow loris gets close, it grabs its prey.

A tarsier grips a slippery trunk with the help of round, flat pads on the ends of its fingers and toes (right). This relative of the loris and of the aye-aye lives in Indonesia and the Philippines. Its powerful legs enable it to leap from tree trunk to tree trunk. When propped against a trunk, its long, hairless tail provides the tarsier with extra support. The tarsier searches at night for insects, lizards, snakes, and small bats and birds to eat.

Small Creatures of the Forest

Plants and animals of the tropical rain forest occupy almost every possible living space. You have seen how some of the larger canopy dwellers have adapted to life among the branches. Many smaller kinds of rain forest animals also have adapted in special ways to life there. In some cases, the animals live within the plants themselves.

A plant called the bromeliad (bro-MEH-lee-add) provides a home for many different kinds of animals. If you were to examine closely the leaves of a single plant, you would find a whole world of creatures hidden there. The bromeliad family of plants includes the familiar pineapple. Many bromeliads grow piggyback on other plants. They take root on tree trunks and large branches, often high off the forest floor. The roots of the bromeliads hold the plants in place. Unlike the roots of many plants, however, these roots do not take in water for the bromeliads. Instead, the long, hard leaves trap water at the bases of the plants.

Small pools form at the bases of the leaves. Spiders, crabs, lizards, frogs, and other animals eat, breed, and find shelter in the pools. Some insects—mosquitoes and dragonflies, for example—lay their

PAUL A. ZAHL, PH.D.

Plants called bromeliads (bro-MEH-lee-adds) grow on a tree limb in a South American rain forest (left). Stiff, overlapping leaves collect rainwater, forming tiny pools inside the plants. The pools become homes for many kinds of small animals.

A cutaway view of a bromeliad plant shows trapped rainwater and the animal life you might find there (right). Dead plant and animal matter has piled up at the bottom of the rainwater pools. This material provides fertilizer for the plant, and food for some of the tiny animals.
1. Tadpoles wriggle in the pool. They hatched from eggs that frogs laid there. As they grow, the tadpoles will feed on bacteria and algae in the water.
2. A red-eyed tree frog peers around a leaf. Water in the plant keeps the frog's skin moist.
3. Lying in wait, a daddy longlegs will pounce on passing mosquitoes and other small insects.
4. A slug inches up a leaf. Like the frog, it depends on water to keep its body damp.
5. Swimming below the surface, a crab searches for mosquito larvae to eat.
6. Mosquito eggs drift at the water surface. Just beneath the surface, hatched mosquito larvae hang upside down in the water.

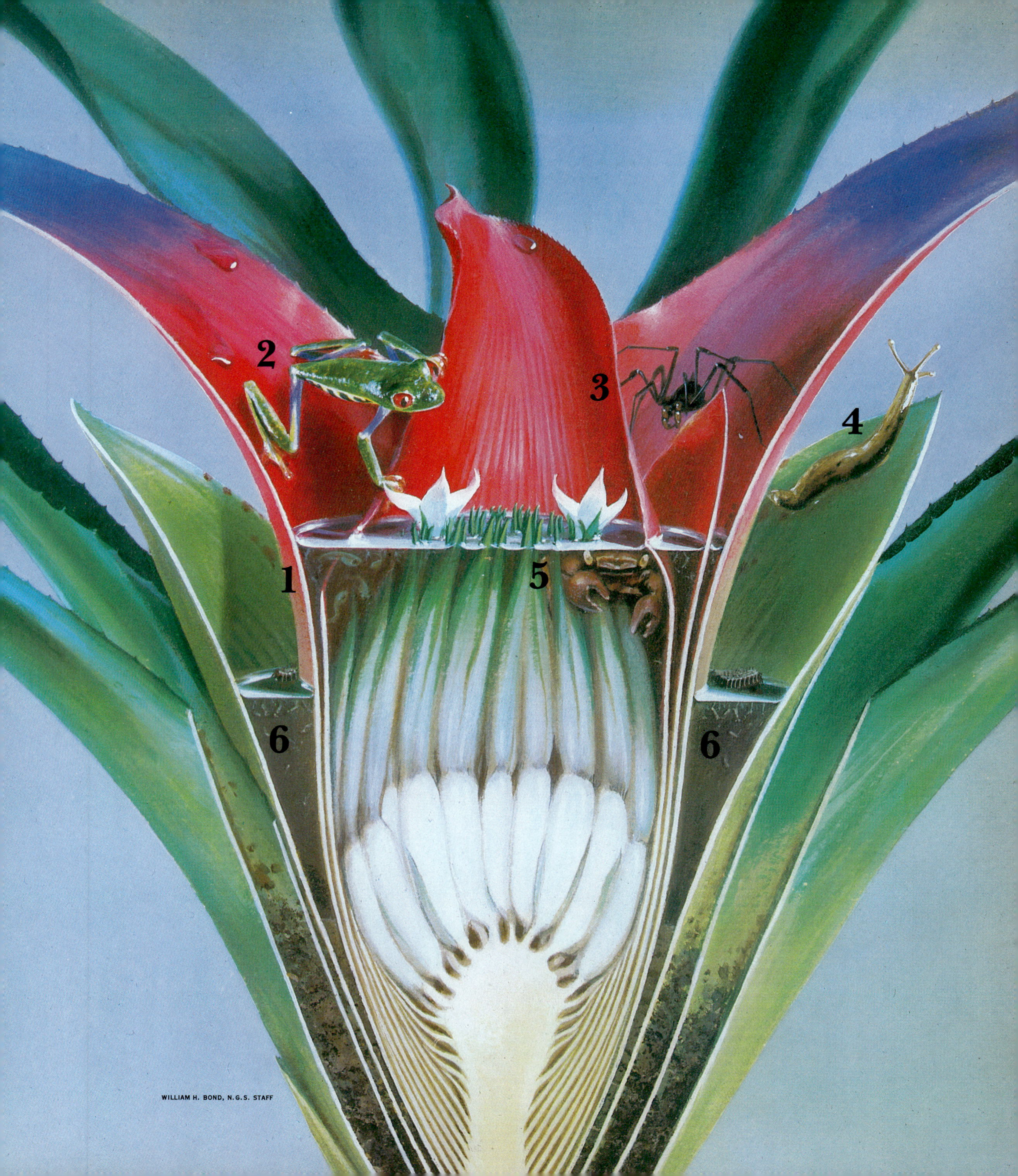
2
3
4
1
5
6
6
WILLIAM H. BOND, N.G.S. STAFF

A red-eyed tree frog crouches on a leaf in Costa Rica, a country in Central America. Pads at the ends of its fingers and toes stick to the leaf. They help the frog move around among the leaves and branches of the rain forest. There, the frog hunts for insects to eat.

CAROL HUGHES

eggs in the tiny pools. Certain frogs may hatch, grow up, and die in a single bromeliad plant.

Of all the small creatures in the rain forest, insects are the most numerous. They fly around, or crawl upon, almost every surface of the biome. Picture yourself walking through a rain forest in Central or South America, searching for insects. Suddenly you come across a wide path that crosses yours. Here, thousands of ants are busily at work. They ignore you as long as you don't bother them. Many of the ants travel in one direction. They carry pieces of leaves that are larger than themselves. Others, without loads, hurry in the opposite direction. These insects are leaf-cutting ants. If you were to guess that the ants were carrying home their food, you'd be wrong. These ants are farmers. They

A South American leaf frog clings to a blossom (above). Look at this picture from across the room. Do the shape and colors of the frog camouflage it?

are carrying home plant material they will use to grow their food.

Leaf-cutting ants live underground in huge groups called colonies. One colony may have several million ants. Every day large worker ants follow well-worn trails from their nests. They mark their trails with chemicals from their bodies. With scissor-like jaws, they snip off bits of leaves from trees and bushes. They may strip bare large portions of a single plant. Then they parade back to the nest holding the pieces in their mouths.

The largest of the workers are called soldier ants. They guard other workers against predators. Soldier ants can bite severely. Once bitten, predators such as lizards are likely to avoid the ants.

Inside the nest, small worker ants cut the leaf pieces into smaller bits. They chew the bits, mixing in their saliva. The chewed leaves turn into a spongy mass. On this mass of plant matter, a particular kind of fungus soon begins to grow. The leaf-cutting ants tend the mixture, fertilizing it with their droppings. The ants eat the fungus as their main food.

EDWARD S. ROSS

PAUL A. ZAHL, PH.D.

A leaf-cutting ant in South America carves a chunk from a leaf (far left). Jagged jaws like those at left cut through the leaf. After snipping off a piece of leaf, the ant will carry it to its nest.

Carrying hefty loads, leaf-cutting ants march along
a vine (above). On a trail they made, ants by the
thousand return to their nest with the pieces of
leaves (left). At the nest, the ants chew the pieces
into fine bits mixed with saliva. They add their
droppings to this mixture, on which a fungus soon
grows. The ants depend on the fungus for food.

CAROL HUGHES

63

Clinging to bark, a Central American tree frog blends with a tree trunk (above). The color and pattern of the frog's warty skin match the bark. This camouflage helps it hide from predators, such as snakes and birds. A katydid, from northern South America, looks almost exactly like a leaf (below). It even has brown spots that resemble leaf rot. By keeping still, it may fool predators.

Helpful Disguises

Hiking along a rain forest path, you'd easily see the leaf-cutting ants you just read about. At close range, they stand out clearly on the forest floor. However, you could be very close to some other kinds of animals and never know it. Many rain forest animals have colors and shapes that make them blend almost perfectly with their surroundings. Blending in allows such animals to avoid detection by predators, or to approach and catch their prey.

Sometimes it's not just an animal's shape or color that hides it. It's also the way the animal behaves. Disguised animals often remain perfectly still. Sudden movements might reveal their presence to enemies—or to prey. The sloth, for example, hangs motionless most of the time on a tree limb. It may look like an insect nest to passing eagles or to hunting cats. Some animals, such as moths, press their bodies close to the branch or trunk where they perch. This helps a camouflaged moth avoid casting a shadow that would give away its presence.

Insects visiting this orchid look-alike (above) are in for a surprise. It's really a white flower mantis, an insect from Southeast Asia. It eats other insects. A vine snake (right), in Central America, looks like just another vine. Frogs and lizards often don't notice the difference—until it's too late.

SAVANNAS

ROBERT CAPUTO

On the African savanna, dry grass waves in the breeze as young cheetahs and their mother watch for antelopes or other prey (above). A cheetah's spotted coat helps it hide in the grass as it approaches its prey.

The savanna, a kind of grassland, covers parts of Africa, South America, Asia, and Australia. Savannas, colored in dark brown (above), usually have trees scattered among the grasses.

Giraffes stride across a savanna in East Africa (left). The tall animals feed mainly on tree leaves. Their height allows them to eat leaves other leaf-eaters cannot reach. Long necks serve as lookout towers. They help the giraffes spot lions far away.

Vast open grasslands called savannas cover many parts of the world. Most lie in tropical regions. Savannas usually have one rainy season. With the rains, thick grass grows quickly. During the rest of the year, the grass dries out and turns golden. Only trees stay green year round.

Large herds of animals, including many kinds of antelopes, live on the savanna. The open grassland offers the herd animals few places to hide. To survive, many depend on keen eyesight. They can spot predators far away. Most can run swiftly, fleeing such predators as cheetahs and lions. Living together in large numbers helps herd animals survive. One animal may spot an enemy and alert the others.

Savanna hunters have keen vision, too. Lions and cheetahs, for example, can spot prey across wide areas of flat savanna. They quietly approach, then dash after their prey on the open land.

Treetop Feeders

In the coolness of early morning, herds of giraffes walk with their young among the trees that dot the African savanna. Standing, the animals tower almost as high as the trees. The giraffes stretch their necks into the treetops and pluck off green leaves with their long tongues and tough lips.

Giraffes grow taller than any other animal in the world. An adult male may reach 18 feet (5½ m). That's almost as tall as a two-story building. Giraffes can reach all but the highest branches. Of the other large animals on the savanna, only elephants can feed on the high tree leaves. The height of giraffes helps them survive, since they compete with so few

animals for the same food. Most of the savanna plant-eaters, such as zebras, graze on grasses. Others, including some rhinoceroses and small antelopes, eat the leaves of low bushes and shrubs.

Giraffes' coats have patterns of brown or tan patches. The patterns blend with the shadows among the trees. This blending may make it hard for lions, their only predators, to see them. Giraffes usually stay near the scattered trees of the savanna. Craning their necks, they watch in all directions for movement. Because their eyes are far above the ground, the giraffes can see a long way, just as you can when you're standing atop a tall tower. Spotting

MARK N. BOULTON/BRUCE COLEMAN LTD.

Reaching high, a giraffe nibbles the leaves of an acacia (uh-KAY-shuh) tree (left). The acacia has sharp thorns, but they can't pierce the giraffe's tough lips. The leaves provide the giraffe with nourishment, and much of the moisture it needs.

LEONARD LEE RUE III

To reach down for a drink, a giraffe must spread its front legs far apart (left). Lions can attack and kill a giraffe in this unguarded position. When standing upright, the giraffe can defend itself by kicking an attacker with its large hooves.

A giraffe stretches out its flexible tongue to feed (above). The tongue may grow as long as 21 inches (54 cm). A giraffe often uses its tongue to pull a branch into its mouth. Then it slides its mouth along the branch, ripping off the leaves.

IAN BEAMES/ARDEA LONDON (OPPOSITE)

an enemy from afar, giraffes can often run away in time to escape. They gallop as fast as 35 miles an hour (56 km/h).

Giraffes drink at water holes. Lions hiding nearby often try to pounce on young giraffes. The young may not be able to defend themselves. However, adult giraffes, usually peaceful and timid, fight fiercely when protecting their young. They can kick hard enough to kill an attacking lion.

Giants With Tusks

African elephants live in herds on the savanna and in forests along the edges of the savanna. Large males sometimes grow as heavy as 13,000 pounds (5,897 kg)—heavier than any other kind of land animal. Elephants keep moving over the savanna all day long, searching for food. Lions, wild dogs, and

An African elephant uses its trunk to pull up reeds (below). The animal also uses its trunk to gather many other kinds of plant food on the savanna, from grasses and fruit to huge tree branches.

An elephant drinks from a pit it has dug (above). During an extra-long hot season, regular water holes may dry up. Then elephants go to dry riverbeds and paw holes in the ground. Using the tips of their trunks like hands, they scoop out soil until underground water seeps into the holes.

hyenas may prey on young elephants that stray from the herd, but adult elephants do not have to fear predators. Their great size protects them. Human hunters with rifles are their main threat.

To support their huge bodies, elephants eat as much as 300 pounds (136 kg) of food a day. They gather and eat every available kind of plant life, including coarse grasses and tree bark.

Elephants use their trunks to gather food and to lift it to their mouths. They pull up large tufts of grass and tear down branches. They sometimes use their foreheads as bulldozers, pushing over trees to get at the leaves at the top.

Elephants use their tusks as well as their trunks to gather food. With their tusks, which are actually enlarged front teeth, the animals dig up big roots and strip bark from trees.

Large grinding teeth, the molars, mash the coarse plant food before it passes to the stomach. Over many years, the molars wear down with use,
but new ones grow in. In a lifetime, an elephant grows six sets of molars.

An elephant's trunk helps the animal survive in many ways other than by gathering food. The trunk is an extension of the nose and the upper lip. An elephant uses its trunk to sniff the wind. It can sniff near the ground, or hold its trunk high in the air. The elephant can detect scents from several hundred yards away. Having weak eyesight, it depends on its nose to find its food.

The elephant's trunk is strong enough to lift heavy logs. Yet the end of the trunk contains delicate muscles and nerves. The enormous animal can pick up small objects such as nuts and berries with the very end of its trunk.

Elephants sometimes use their trunks as big straws. They suck in water, then squirt it into their mouths. They may fill their trunks with as much as a gallon and a half (6 L) of water, and spray it over their bodies in a cooling shower.

As butterflies sip moisture, dung beetles feed on elephant dung—solid waste matter (right). The beetles make use of the dung in another way, too. Below, a beetle rolls a dung ball before burying it. After the ball is buried, a female beetle lays an egg in the ball. The dung provides food for the larva that hatches. The dung also helps fertilize the soil.

A painting of a cut-open dung ball shows a dung beetle larva inside (left). The larva feeds on the dung. Like a cocoon, the buried dung ball protects the insect from the savanna heat until it comes out as an adult.

Grounded Birds

When robins and most other birds have to escape, they fly. They can run, but not fast enough to escape most enemies. Some kinds of birds on the savanna cannot fly at all. Their wings will not support them. The largest of these, the ostrich of Africa, may weigh as much as 300 pounds (136 kg). You might wonder how such a heavy bird could escape from danger on the ground. If you tried to chase an ostrich, you'd see how it survives without flying.

An ostrich can run across flat grasslands about as fast as a racehorse. At full speed, it can cross a narrow dirt road in one step. To lure a hungry lion or other attacker away from its nest, an ostrich may zigzag rapidly across the ground. It can run for as long as 30 minutes without slowing down. An ostrich's foot has two strong toes with hard nails. When the bird runs, it digs its toes into the ground to push itself quickly along.

In addition to speed, the ostrich relies on alertness to survive. Its sharp eyes, like the giraffe's, are high above the ground. The ostrich can see far across the flat plains, watching for signs of danger.

The ostrich lays its eggs in a shallow nest on the ground. The male and female take turns sitting on the eggs to keep them warm. The female has light brown or gray feathers. The male has black feathers. During the day, the female bird sits on the nest. Her feathers blend with the ground, hiding the nest from predators. The male sits on the nest at night. His black feathers hide the nest in the dark.

The birds below may look alike, but they are not closely related. The ostrich lives in Africa; the rhea (REE-uh), in South America; and the emu (EE-mew), in Australia. Although the birds live far apart, all three have developed similar ways of surviving on savannas. None of them can fly. With long legs and strong toes, all run fast across the grasslands.

Rhea

Emu

Ostrich

Followed by her chicks, an ostrich struts on the savanna in Kenya, in East Africa. Spreading her wings helps her cool off in the breeze. The ostrich cannot fly, but an adult can often run fast enough to escape from a lion, its main enemy.

Patas monkeys rest on a fallen tree (above). On their long legs, these monkeys of the African savanna run swiftly through the grass to flee leopards and other predators. In the dry season, the grass will turn golden. The color of the monkeys' hair will camouflage the animals as they hunt for food.

Grassland Monkeys

Most monkeys live in forests. They find food and safety in the trees. But some monkeys live on the savanna, where trees are widely scattered. These monkeys spend much of their lives on the ground.

Patas monkeys live on the African savanna. They travel in groups. One male leads a group of about 15 females and young. All day long, they search for fruit, insects, and other food. The monkeys sometimes climb trees to rest. But to flee danger in the savanna, they usually have to run across the ground. With long, thin bodies and long legs, the monkeys dart through the tall grass. They run on the ground faster than any other monkeys.

While the females and young feed, the male patas monkey acts as a guard and watches for danger. Sharp-eyed and alert, he stands up on his hind legs and peers over the grass to watch for enemies, such as the leopard. If a predator comes near, the male dashes out to catch its attention. Running swiftly, he leads the attacker far off so the females and the young can run silently to safety.

Among baboons, several males guard a troop as it feeds and travels. The large male baboons watch for wild dogs, leopards, and other predators. If an enemy approaches, the male baboons join forces against it. They snarl and show their long, pointed teeth. The baboons can kill an attacker with these daggerlike fangs. Usually, they don't have to. The predator backs off, scared away by the sight of so many sharp teeth.

On the savanna in Kenya, olive baboons search for tender grasses as well as insects and other small animals to eat (right). Baboons live mostly on the ground, in troops. A troop may have as many as 80 animals. Large males guard the other baboons. They can frighten away or defeat most attackers, such as hyenas. A young baboon (below) rides on its mother's back. It stays close to her for safety until it is several months old.

Built for Speed

Cheetahs depend on super speed and excellent eyesight for survival. In seconds, a cheetah can sprint from a standing position to almost 60 miles an hour (97 km/h). This lanky cat of the African savanna has long legs and a flexible spine. Together, they allow the cheetah to stretch out and run as fast as it does.

Cheetahs often climb onto large mounds to look for prey. They hunt mostly antelopes. When a cheetah sees a herd, it stalks the animals, approaching slowly and silently. Antelopes often don't notice a cheetah's tan, spotted coat in the savanna grass.

Usually, cheetahs stalk as close as possible before they attack. They look for an animal that is separated from the herd. The cheetah gets within about 100 feet (30 m) of its prey. Then, with a lightning burst of speed, the cat streaks after its target. The cheetah knocks down the antelope with its powerful front feet. On each front foot, the cheetah has one claw that doesn't touch the ground. These claws, called dewclaws, are needle sharp. They help the cheetah knock down its prey. The cheetah kills by biting its victim's throat.

Cheetahs often do not catch their intended prey. The cheetahs can run faster than antelopes, but they can't run as far. Cheetahs run at top speed for only short distances, and then they tire. If a cheetah does not catch its prey quickly, it gives up and rests for another attempt later.

Fastest of all land animals, cheetahs close in on a small antelope called a Thomson's gazelle (right). They will try to pounce on it for a midmorning meal. A lone cheetah (below) lopes across the savanna in East Africa. Cheetahs depend largely on speed to catch prey. Over short distances, they can run at almost 60 miles an hour (97 km/h).

In southern Africa (above), two trees grow from a termite mound. Termites mix sand and soil with their own saliva to build such a tower. Home for millions of termites, it may rise 20 feet (6 m).

World of Termites

Tall mounds of hardened mud rise from the African savanna. Tiny builders—termites—constructed them. Sometimes millions of termites live in a single mound. It may tower as high as 20 feet (6 m). To build a mound, the termites make a sticky cement of soil and sand mixed with their saliva. The thick walls, as hard as baked clay, help protect the soft-skinned termites from predators outside, and from the hot, dry savanna air.

The interior of a termite mound contains many rooms and tunnels. In some rooms, the termites store food. In others, they care for termite eggs and young. The queen, far bigger than any of the other termites, lives with a mate in a chamber deep inside the mound. She does nothing but lay eggs. She may lay 30,000 eggs a day. Worker termites feed and care for the queen and her mate. The workers also gather food for the rest of the colony and build and repair the mound.

Termites are sensitive to heat and dryness. Too much heat or dryness would kill them quickly. Inside the mound, the termites have their own air-conditioning system. They build networks of tunnels running up and down the insides of the mound

Worker termites drag home a blade of grass (above). After chewing and partly digesting it, they will feed the grass to other termites in the colony. Workers also build and repair the mound.

Inside a mound (above), worker termites care for the young, which are white. Other workers repair a broken wall with mud. A termite mound opened by scientists reveals long tunnels (right). These tunnels circulate air inside the mound. The fresh air brings the oxygen the termites need, and it cools them.

An aardvark in Kenya sniffs a termite mound at night. Aardvarks break open termite mounds and eat the insects inside. To find termites in the dark, they rely on their keen senses of smell and hearing.

walls. They can open these tunnels to let in cooler outside air when the air inside has become too hot. The thick mound walls help hold in moisture from the soil below.

Termites feed on wood, fungus, grass, and other coarse plant material. They cannot digest this food themselves. Microscopic animals living in the bodies of the termites help them digest it.

While worker termites build a mound, other termites, called soldier termites, protect the colony from small enemies, especially ants. Soldier termites have large, pointed jaws. They use these as biting and slashing weapons to fight off ants that invade the mound to eat the termites.

Although termites can fight off other insects, they cannot fight off some larger predators, such as the aardvark. The aardvark's tough hide protects it from the bites of soldier termites.

In the Afrikaans language of South Africa, "aardvark" means "earth pig." Because of its long snout, the aardvark looks somewhat like a pig. But it is not related to the pig.

The aardvark sniffs along the ground to find termite mounds at night. When it finds a mound, it digs a hole in the base with the sharp claws on its front feet. The claws are so strong that an aardvark can rip a whole mound apart in a night. To catch termites, the aardvark pokes out its long tongue, which is covered with mucus. Some termites stick to the sticky substance and quickly become a meal.

Digging with its strong claws, an aardvark tunnels into a termite mound (left). The sunbaked walls may be almost as hard as bricks. But aardvarks have little trouble breaking through. Once inside, they use their long tongues to catch the termites.

As an aardvark digs, nose bristles (right) filter dust from the air the animal breathes. The aardvark relies on its senses of hearing and smell to avoid enemies, such as wild dogs. To flee, an aardvark may quickly burrow underground. If attacked, it rolls over and slashes with its claws.

ANIMALS ANIMALS/HANS AND JUDY BESTE

Sharp spines protect the echidna (ih-KID-nuh) from enemies (left). This Australian animal, also called a spiny anteater, preys on ants, termites, and other insects. Like the aardvark, it uses sharp claws to dig into insect nests. It also has a long tongue covered with mucus. The echidna darts its tongue into insect nests. Then it draws back the tongue and swallows the insects that stick to it.

Red kangaroos in eastern Australia (above) use their muscular tails to balance themselves. A red kangaroo (left) springs on powerful hind legs. It can leap as high as 10 feet (3 m) and travel as far as 25 feet (8 m) in one bound.

Long-distance Hoppers

Red kangaroos live on dry, grassy plains in much of Australia. Among the largest of all kangaroos, these animals grow as tall as a tall basketball player. Red kangaroos feed on the grasses that grow on the plains. To find enough food, they travel long distances every day.

To walk along slowly, a kangaroo leans forward and rests all of its weight on its front feet and on its tail. Then it swings its hind feet forward under its body. To move fast, however, a kangaroo leaps. A fast-moving kangaroo touches the ground with only its hind legs.

A red kangaroo has long, powerful hind legs. It can leap as fast as 40 miles an hour (64 km/h). Moving fast helps it escape enemies, such as wild dogs called dingoes. Leaping is an easy way to travel. Scientists recently found that a leaping animal uses less energy than a similar-size running animal does.

The maned wolf (right) lives on the pampas, or grasslands, of South America. Long legs give it a view over the grass. Another pampas animal, a rodent called a mara (muh-RAH or MAH-ruh), searches for food with her young (below). Their long ears pick up the faintest sounds of enemies.

JEN AND DES BARTLETT

Long-legged Runners

Savanna grasslands called the pampas stretch across parts of South America. The pampas are home to the tallest of the wild dogs—the maned wolf. This slender animal looks more like a fox than like a wolf. That fact, and its long legs, earned it the nickname "fox on stilts." The maned wolf hunts insects, birds, reptiles, and small mammals, such as rabbits. It also eats fruit. The wolf can rush at high speed across the pampas when chasing prey.

Another long-legged animal, called the mara (muh-RAH or MAH-ruh), lives on the pampas. This large rodent looks a bit like a hare, but the mara actually is related to the guinea pig. To flee an enemy, such as a fox, the mara runs, bounding fast, touching the ground with all four feet at once. Thick pads and hair under the feet protect its paws from the rough ground. As it runs, the mara displays a patch of white hair on its rump. This patch may warn other maras of danger.

ANIMALS ANIMALS/L. L. T. RHODES (RIGHT)

MOUNTAINS

JEFF FOOTT/BRUCE COLEMAN INC.

Tumbled rocks help protect a pika (PEA-kuh or PIE-kuh) high on a slope in the Rocky Mountains (above). The pika uses spaces among rocks to store food, to escape from such predators as hawks, and to avoid icy winds.

Mountainous regions are shaded in dark blue (above). Some mountains rise close to the seashore. Others lie inland on high plateaus.

On the edge of a rocky drop-off in northern Italy, one male alpine ibex (EYE-becks) rears playfully next to another (left). Ibexes live for most of the year on steep slopes high in the mountains. They graze on patches of grass among the rocks.

Mountains. The word may make you think of windswept ice near the top of Mount Everest. Or perhaps it makes you imagine a sunny picnic by a lake in the Rocky Mountains. Or maybe you picture a shady pine grove on a gentle slope in Virginia. Each image is accurate. Mountains differ widely. Some have high, treeless, frozen peaks. Others have windy summits with alpine meadows. Some have rounded, forested tops.

Just about all mountains do have one thing in common. The air becomes colder as you climb toward the summit. As the air becomes colder, the kinds of plant and animal life change. On most mountains, you'll find different zones of plant and animal life as you go up. Trees grow shorter at higher elevations. If you go high enough, you'll leave the trees behind altogether. But you'll probably still find quite a few animals—like those in this chapter.

JEAN-PAUL FERRERO/ARDEA LONDON (OPPOSITE)

After grazing on plants, Spanish ibexes chew their food high on a mountainside in Spain. As they chew, they rest on steep slopes, watching for predators such as eagles. Hard, rough pads under their hooves help the ibexes walk on steep rocks and along cliff edges without slipping. All ibexes grow horns. Only the males grow horns that become great pointed curves.

Hooves in the Heights

The early spring sun rises over the Swiss Alps. A cold breeze brushes the treetops on a mountainside. About 15 female ibexes (EYE-beck-sez) and their kids graze on the slope near the edge of the forest. The trees shade them. Soon, one of the adults leads the herd higher. They leave the forest for a part of the slope where no trees grow. Here, much of the snow has blown away. The remaining white blanket has begun to melt. The group heads for plants and resting places high among cliffs bathed by the sun. Close to their mothers, the kids leap playfully.

The herd zigzags its way up a rocky cliff wall. Suddenly, a golden eagle swoops down from the sky. It dives at a small kid. As the eagle nears its prey, the closest adult rears up and butts at the large bird. The eagle swerves, just out of reach. Then it soars off to hunt elsewhere.

During the coldest parts of the winter, ibexes spend the days among the trees at the upper edges

RENÉ-PIERRE BILLE

A chamois (SHAM-ee) charges across snow in the mountains of Italy (above). When undisturbed, the chamois grazes quietly. But to flee enemies, it races across rough, rocky ground with ease.

of the slopes. For the rest of the year, they live among the highest ledges of the mountains, looking down into valleys thousands of feet below.

Climbing among rocks presents no problem to ibexes. Their split hooves have hard but flexible pads. The pads help prevent slipping on rocky surfaces. Hard outside edges and hoof tips grow beyond the pads. The hoof edges and tips catch on bumps and cracks in the rocks. The combination of pads and hard edges allows the ibexes to climb and jump among the steepest rocks and narrowest ledges without falling.

The ibex shares its hoof design with other mountain animals. The mountain goat, chamois (SHAM-ee), and bighorn sheep all have similar hooves—and climb equally well. Powerful hindquarters help these animals leap to higher rock ledges. They bound across cracks too wide for predators to follow easily. Few predators chase wild goats and sheep among rocky mountaintops.

Another kind of hoofed mountain dweller, an antelope called the klipspringer, lives in parts of Africa on mountain slopes covered with boulders. Leaping from boulder to boulder, a klipspringer can land on the tips of its hooves on a spot no bigger than a doorknob. The klipspringer has brittle hair that pulls out easily. A biting predator, such as a leopard, may get only a mouthful of hair. The klipspringer escapes—frightened but alive.

Standing on the tips of its hard, rubberlike hooves, a klipspringer looks out over a rocky slope in East Africa (above). This small antelope often escapes predators by springing from boulder to boulder.

A young Rocky Mountain goat straddles a deep split in a mountain wall (below). An expert climber, the goat lives among rocky peaks in western North America. A woolly undercoat keeps away extreme cold. Outer guard hairs shed rain and snow.

A Rocky Mountain bighorn sheep crosses a cliff face in Montana. Enemies such as coyotes cannot easily attack the sheep here. Like ibexes, the bighorn has hooves with hard edges and hard, rough pads. These features allow the sheep to use any small crack or rocky edge when crossing a steep area. In the coldest months, the sheep find sunny slopes for warmth.

A herd of vicuñas (vi-KOON-yuhs) makes its way through a field of large rocks. Vicuñas live on the high plains of the Andes, mountains in South America. Their thickly padded feet securely grip uneven, rocky surfaces. At high altitudes, air has less oxygen than does air at lower altitudes. Vicuñas get sufficient oxygen with the help of an extra supply of red blood cells. The red blood cells pick up oxygen as blood flows through the lungs.

FRANÇOIS GOHIER/ARDEA LONDON

Two Ways of Spending the Winter

When autumn approaches in the mountains, many of the leaves begin to change color. The daily lives of some mountain animals change, too. Pikas (PEA-kuhs or PIE-kuhs), small animals of western North America and Asia, begin hurrying about, cutting, drying, and storing plants they will eat in winter.

Most pikas live on mountain slopes among large areas of broken rocks, called talus (TAY-lus). The animals remain active, even after snow arrives. Pikas run across snow to eat plants growing at the edge of the talus. When snow buries these plants, the pikas tunnel under the snow to their piles of stored food. This supply lasts all winter.

Pikas have rounded bodies and short legs and ears. They expose less body surface to the cold than they would if they had long ears and long legs. Less exposure helps them hold in their body heat.

At the edge of the talus, on high meadows of Europe, North America, and Asia, marmots stay busy, too. These large, furry rodents don't store food for the winter, however. They eat it as they find it. All spring and summer, marmots eat plants that grow in the meadows around their burrows. They dig these burrows with the curved claws on their strong front feet. By autumn, the marmots have grown so fat that they drag their bellies on the ground. Around the time of the first snow, they enter their burrows, curl up in grass-lined nests, and hibernate. To survive during winter hibernation, they depend on their large stores of body fat.

JEFF FOOTT

A pika gathers herbs on a mountain in western Canada (left). Pikas, small relatives of rabbits and hares, live among rocks near high meadows. They stay active all year. In late summer, they gather grasses and herbs, and store them in huge piles that dry as hay. In winter (right), a pika tunnels through snow to eat from its hay pile.

NATUR-FOTO/ROBERT SPÖNLEIN

Common in high mountains of Europe, an alpine marmot pauses and looks around at its burrow entrance (left). Marmots also live in mountains of North America and Asia. If a marmot sees an eagle or other predator, it whistles. The piercing sound carries far, even on a windy mountainside. Whistling warns other marmots, and other nearby animals, of the danger. The marmot spends much of the day sunning or eating plants near its burrow. When fall comes, the animal will have grown fat. Unlike the pika, the marmot hibernates. Its stored body fat keeps it alive all winter.

The Andean condor (above) of South America's western mountains can soar for hours on rising currents of warm air. Fingerlike feathers at its wing tips help the condor steer without flapping.

Wings spread wide, one Andean condor prepares for takeoff (right). Ocean breezes against the cliff face will help the bird launch itself. Soaring high, the condor can spot food far below on the ground.

High Gliders

Steep cliffs of the Andes face the Pacific Ocean along the western coast of South America. Strong, warm breezes blow toward the cliffs and rise along their walls. The Andean condor, one of the world's largest flying birds, lives among the cliffs. An adult condor weighs about 25 pounds (11 kg). Despite its weight, the condor is a master at soaring. It leaps off a cliff face into the rising breezes. With wings spread as wide as 10 feet (3 m), it can soar for hours. Making use of rising warm-air currents, the condor rarely has to flap its wings.

The condor, a kind of vulture, both roosts and nests on the cliff walls. Like other vultures, it has sharp long-distance eyesight. As it soars, it can spot food on the ground from high in the sky. The condor searches for carrion—the remains of dead animals—to eat. Large numbers of condors often collect when they find carrion. They clean the bodies right down to the skeletons. The condor has no feathers on its head and neck. This allows it to tear off large chunks of meat without getting its feathers messy or matted. The condor's powerful beak is strong enough even to rip through the tough skin of a sea lion it may find on the beach. The bird eats meat many other animals will not eat. In this way, it helps to clean the land of dead animals.

Mountain Hunter

Among the broken boulders that make up its home, the spotted, light-colored snow leopard blends right in. Although well camouflaged, the leopard has been hunted for centuries for its soft, thick fur. This large cat now roams only in a few parts of the mountains of Central Asia. As high as 18,000 feet (5,486 m) above sea level, the snow leopard lives among boulders and snow on steep slopes. It remains alone, except at mating time in the fall.

The snow leopard stays in the high mountains almost all year round. Its thick coat protects it from the extreme cold. The heavily furred cat usually rests and suns itself during the day. It stalks wild sheep, wild goats, deer, and hares—mostly at night. The leopard can follow prey swiftly across snowbanks and up cliffs. Its long tail helps the cat balance as it twists and leaps during a chase. After it kills its prey and eats, the snow leopard may drag the remains to a spot between boulders. There, it stores the food for a later meal.

Jagged patterns formed by snow on dark boulders help hide a snow leopard (left). This large cat lives high in the mountains of Central Asia. In winter, it descends to lower slopes to find prey, such as ibexes.

GARY MILBURN/TOM STACK & ASSOCIATES

GEORGE B. SCHALLER

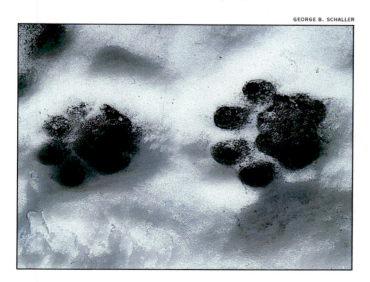

Paw prints in the snow (above) are often all that can be seen of the rare and shy snow leopard. This large cat hunts alone most of the year.

A snow leopard's pale eyes search for prey (above). Like snowshoes, this cat's large, furry feet help it cross snow without sinking in. In winter, as prey struggles in deep snow, the leopard can chase it on the surface of the snow—and often catch it.

GEORGE B. SCHALLER/BRUCE COLEMAN INC. (OPPOSITE)

Forest Mountaineers

In the mountains of Japan, frequent fog and rain keep the forests wet and green much of the year. But this is no tropical rain forest. In winter, snow blankets the ground and the trees. If you were to hike in this cold environment, you might be surprised to spot a troop of . . . monkeys!

Japanese macaques (muh-KACKS), or snow monkeys, live farther north, and in a colder climate, than any other kind of monkey. The hairy coat of Japanese macaques is thicker than the hair of other monkeys. The hair keeps them warm in winter. Macaques eat leaves, fruit, and insects much of the year. This food, however, becomes difficult to find in winter. Then macaques sometimes eat tree bark.

Another dweller of Asian mountains lives on the mainland—in the central part of the People's Republic of China. The giant panda munches the leaves, shoots, and stems of bamboo almost all day long. The panda holds the bamboo in its specially adapted forepaws (see the drawing at the bottom of this page). When the panda takes a bite, its bumpy-surfaced back teeth go to work. They crunch the bamboo into digestible shreds. The giant panda's abilities to hold bamboo and to chew it are two of the animal's secrets of survival.

On a sunny rock, a Japanese macaque (muh-KACK) cuddles her four-month-old (below). Another youngster sits alongside, scratching through its coat of long, thick hair. Japanese macaques, or snow monkeys, live in mountain forests of Japan. In winter, snow covers the forests. The long, thick hair of macaques keeps them warm.

ANIMALS ANIMALS/KOJO TANAKA

A giant panda (right) sits high on a tree branch. It lives on mountain slopes in a part of the People's Republic of China. Bamboo is its main food.

GEORGE B. SCHALLER (BELOW AND OPPOSITE)

Biting into bamboo, a giant panda begins a meal (above). The panda breaks the stem with its teeth, then peels off the tough outer husk. The panda's forepaws are specially adapted for handling bamboo. A long wristbone serves almost as a thumb (arrow, right), helping the panda hold the smooth stems.

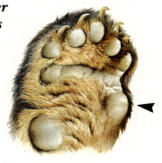

INDEX

Bold type refers to illustrations; regular type refers to text.

STEPHEN J. KRASEMANN/DRK PHOTO

Female Rocky Mountain bighorn sheep stand on an overlook in western Canada. Females' horns are short and gently curved. Males grow long, curled horns.

ADDITIONAL READING

Readers may want to check the *National Geographic Index* in a school or a public library for related articles and to refer to the following books. ("A" indicates a book for readers at the adult level.)

General: Hopf, Alice L., *Nature's Pretenders,* Putnam, 1979. Johnson, Sylvia A., *The Wildlife Atlas,* Lerner Publications, 1977. Leen, Nina, *Monkeys,* Holt, Rinehart & Winston, 1978. *The Marvels of Animal Behavior,* National Geographic Society, 1972 (A). *National Geographic Book of Mammals,* Vols. 1 and 2, National Geographic Society, 1981. Patent, Dorothy Hinshaw, *Hunters and the Hunted: Surviving in the Animal World,* Holiday House, 1981. Stuart, Gene S., *Wildlife Alert! The Struggle to Survive,* National Geographic Society, 1980. Walter, Eugene J., Jr., *Why Animals Behave the Way They Do,* Scribner's, 1981. *Wild Animals of North America,* National Geographic Society, 1979 (A). Wolf, Joyce, *Ants to Zebras: Relationships in Nature,* Julian Messner, 1981.

Polar Regions: Burton, Robert, *Seals,* McGraw-Hill, 1979. Davids, Richard C., *Lords of the Arctic,* Macmillan, 1982 (A). Hopf, Alice L., *Biography of an American Reindeer,* Putnam, 1976. McDearmon, Kay, *Polar Bear,* Dodd, Mead, 1976. Rau, Margaret, *Musk Oxen,* Crowell, 1976. Stonehouse, Bernard, *Animals of the Antarctic,* Holt, Rinehart & Winston, 1972. Stonehouse, Bernard, *Animals of the Arctic,* Holt, Rinehart & Winston, 1972. Tenaza, Richard, *Penguins,* Franklin Watts, 1980. Todd, Frank S., *The Sea World Book of Penguins,* Sea World Press, 1981.

Deserts: Bare, Colleen Stanley, *Rabbits and Hares,* Dodd, Mead, 1983. Cloudsley-Thompson, John, *Camels,* Raintree, 1980. Gauthier-Pilters, Hilde, and Anne Innis Dagg, *The Camel,* University of Chicago Press, 1981 (A). Graham, Ada and Frank, *The Changing Desert,* Scribner's, 1981. Pitt, Valerie, and David Cook, *A Closer Look at Deserts,* Franklin Watts, 1975. Tate, Ro, *Desert Animals,* Harper & Row, 1971 (A). Waters, John F., *Camels: Ships of the Desert,* Crowell, 1974. Young, Donald, *The Great American Desert,* Julian Messner, 1980.

Rain Forests: Amon, Aline, *Orangutan: Endangered Ape,* Atheneum, 1977. Hoke, John, *Discovering the World of the Three-Toed Sloth,* Franklin Watts, 1976. Pope, Joyce, *A Closer Look at Jungles,* Gloucester Press, 1978. Richards, Paul W., *The Life of the Jungle,* McGraw-Hill, 1970.

Savannas: Burton, Jane, *Animals of the African Year,* Holt, Rinehart & Winston, 1972. De la Fuente, Felix Rodriguez, *Hunters and Hunted of the Savannah,* Orbis Publishing, 1970 (A). Eaton, Randall L., *The Cheetah: Nature's Fastest Racer,* Dodd, Mead, 1981. Frame, George and Lory, *Swift and Enduring: Cheetahs and Wild Dogs of the Serengeti,* Dutton, 1981 (A). Horton, Catherine, *A Closer Look at Grasslands,* Gloucester Press, 1979. MacClintock, Dorcas, *A Natural History of Giraffes,* Scribner's, 1973. Overbeck, Cynthia, *Elephants,* Lerner Publications, 1981. Rau, Margaret, *The Gray Kangaroo at Home,* Knopf, 1978. Schaller, George and Kay, *Wonders of Lions,* Dodd, Mead, 1977. Schick, Alice, *Serengeti Cats,* Lippincott, 1977. Van Wormer, Joe, *Elephants,* Dutton, 1976. Williamson, H. D., *The Year of the Kangaroo,* Scribner's, 1977. Wrogemann, Nan, *Cheetah Under the Sun,* McGraw-Hill, 1975 (A).

Mountains: Conklin, Gladys, *The Llamas of South America,* Holiday House, 1975. Long, Tony, *Mountain Animals,* Harper & Row, 1971 (A). McDearmon, Kay, *Rocky Mountain Bighorns,* Dodd, Mead, 1980. Orr, Robert T., *The Little-Known Pika,* Macmillan, 1977 (A). Perry, Roger, *Wonders of Llamas,* Dodd, Mead, 1977. Rau, Margaret, *The Giant Panda at Home,* Knopf, 1977. Rau, Margaret, *The Snow Monkey at Home,* Knopf, 1979. Ricciuti, Edward R., *Wildlife of the Mountains,* Abrams, 1979 (A).

CONSULTANTS

William A. Xanten, Jr., National Zoological Park, *Chief Consultant*
Glenn O. Blough, LL.D., University of Maryland, *Educational Consultant*
Lynda Ehrlich, Montgomery County (Maryland) Public Schools, *Reading Consultant*
Phyllis G. Sidorsky, National Cathedral School, *Consulting Librarian*
Nicholas J. Long, Ph.D., *Consulting Psychologist*

The Special Publications and School Services Division is grateful to the individuals and organizations listed here for their generous cooperation and assistance during the preparation of SECRETS OF ANIMAL SURVIVAL:

Claud A. Bramblett, University of Texas at Austin; Dewey Caron, University of Delaware; Garrett C. Clough, Nasson College; Ronald I. Crombie, Smithsonian Institution; Robert DeFillips, Smithsonian Institution; Eric Edney, University of British Columbia; Louise H. Emmons, Smithsonian Institution; George W. Frame; Valerius Geist, University of Calgary; David R. Gray, National Museums of Canada; William J. Hamilton III, University of California at Davis; David Hancocks, Woodland Park Zoological Gardens.

Jessica A. Harrison, Smithsonian Institution; Wybrand Hoek, Fisheries and Oceans Canada, Arctic Biological Station; Robert S. Hoffmann, University of Kansas; Devra Kleiman, National Zoological Park; Stewart D. MacDonald, National Museums of Canada; Wilbur W. Mayhew, University of California at Riverside; David E. Murrish, State University of New York at Binghamton; Robert D. Ohmart, Arizona State University; Robert T. Orr, California Academy of Sciences; Oliver Pearson, University of California at Berkeley; Charles W. Pickett, National Zoological Park; David and Virginia Pratt; Glenn Prestwich, State University of New York at Stony Brook; Brett C. Ratcliffe, University of Nebraska; Robert W. Read, Smithsonian Institution.

Jon Rood, Conservation and Research Center, National Zoological Park; Henry W. Setzer, Curator of Mammals, Emeritus, Smithsonian Institution; Jeheskel (Hezy) Shoshani, Elephant Interest Group, Wayne State University; Noel Snyder, U. S. Fish and Wildlife Service; Mel and Fiona Sunquist, University of Florida; Ian Tattersall, American Museum of Natural History; Richard W. Thorington, Jr., Smithsonian Institution; Paul C. Tirrell, State University of New York at Binghamton; Neal A. Weber, Florida State University; Ralph M. Wetzel, University of Florida; Ron Wilhelm, Environmental Protection Agency.

Composition for SECRETS OF ANIMAL SURVIVAL by National Geographic's Photographic Services, Carl M. Shrader, Director; Lawrence F. Ludwig, Assistant Director. Printed and bound by Holladay-Tyler Printing Corp., Rockville, Md. Color separations by the Lanman-Progressive Co., Washington, D. C.; Lincoln Graphics, Inc., Cherry Hill, N.J.; NEC, Inc., Nashville, Tenn. Classroom Activities folder produced by Mazer Corp., Dayton, Ohio.

Library of Congress CIP Data
Main entry under title:
Secrets of animal survival.
(Books for world explorers)
Includes index.
SUMMARY: Describes the specific physical adaptations of animals to five different types of environments including Arctic and Antarctic, desert, rain forest, savanna, and mountain.
1. Animal behavior—Juvenile literature. 2. Adaptation (Physiology)—Juvenile literature. [1. Animals—Habitations. 2. Animals—Habits and behavior. 3. Adaptation (Biology)] I. Series.
QL751.5.S53 1983   591.5   81-47895
ISBN 0-87044-426-3 (regular binding)
ISBN 0-87044-431-X (library binding)

SECRETS OF ANIMAL SURVIVAL

PUBLISHED BY
THE NATIONAL GEOGRAPHIC SOCIETY
WASHINGTON, D. C.

Gilbert M. Grosvenor, *President*
Melvin M. Payne, *Chairman of the Board*
Owen R. Anderson, *Executive Vice President*
Robert L. Breeden, *Vice President, Publications and Educational Media*

PREPARED BY THE SPECIAL PUBLICATIONS
AND SCHOOL SERVICES DIVISION

Donald J. Crump, *Director*
Philip B. Silcott, *Associate Director*
William L. Allen, William R. Gray, *Assistant Directors*

STAFF FOR BOOKS FOR WORLD EXPLORERS

Ralph Gray, *Editor*
Pat Robbins, *Managing Editor*
Ursula Perrin Vosseler, *Art Director*

STAFF FOR *SECRETS OF ANIMAL SURVIVAL*
Roger B. Hirschland, *Managing Editor*
Veronica J. Morrison, *Picture Editor*
Louise Ponsford, *Designer*
Robert E. Hynes, *Artist*
Sharon L. Barry (Rain Forests), Deb Bennett (Mountains), Judith E. Rinard (Polar Regions, Deserts, Savannas), *Writers*
Debra A. Antonini, Mary B. Campbell, *Researchers*
Joan Hurst, *Editorial Assistant*
Artemis S. Lampathakis, *Illustrations Assistant*
Janet A. Dustin, *Art Secretary*
John D. Garst, Jr., Patricia K. Cantlay, Judith Bell Siegel, *Map Research and Production*

STAFF FOR *FAR-OUT FUN!* Patricia N. Holland, *Project Editor;* Ross Bankson, *Text Editor;* Louise Ponsford, *Designer;* Debra A. Antonini, Mary B. Campbell, *Researchers;* Dru Colbert, *Artist*

ENGRAVING, PRINTING,
AND PRODUCT MANUFACTURE
Robert W. Messer, *Manager;* George V. White, *Production Manager;* Mark R. Dunlevy, Gregory Storer, *Production Project Managers;* Richard A. McClure, David V. Showers, *Assistant Production Managers;* Katherine H. Donohue, *Senior Production Assistant;* Mary A. Bennett, *Production Assistant;* Julia F. Warner, *Production Staff Assistant*

STAFF ASSISTANTS: Nancy F. Berry, Pamela A. Black, Mary Elizabeth Davis, Rosamund Garner, Victoria D. Garrett, Jane R. Halpin, Nancy J. Harvey, Rebecca Bittle Johns, Katherine R. Leitch, Virginia W. McCoy, Mary Evelyn McKinney, Cleo Petroff, Tammy Presley, Sheryl A. Prohovich, Carol A. Rocheleau, Kathleen T. Shea

MARKET RESEARCH: Mark W. Brown, Joseph S. Fowler, Carrla L. Holmes, Meg McElligott Kieffer, Nancy Serbin, Susan D. Snell, Barbara G. Steinwurtzel

INDEX: Jeffrey A. Brown